STEAM MEMORIES: 1950's – 1960's

No. 79: NORTHUMBERLAND BRA

DAVID DUNN

Copyright Book Law Publications 2017
ISBN 978-1-909625-75-4

Welcome to the first of a trilogy of albums featuring the branch lines of Northumberland. This album will feature the following lines: Alston from Haltwhistle; the Amble branch; the Avenue branch; Chathill–Seahouses (North Sunderland Railway); and the Newbiggin branch. For those of you familiar with the lines you will note that one is inland whilst the others are near or on the coast. To give you the best coverage possible we have included a few images from the LNER post-war years so our own 'mini title' *1950s-1960s* has been 'stretched' somewhat in order to accommodate these superb images which do not detract in any way and certainly enhance the illustrations.

The subjects of this first album contain much in the way of 'material' and ideas for modellers, besides enthusiasts and historians. It is often forgotten that other areas of Britain had picturesque branch lines beside the GWR. Northumberland was full of them offering every type situation and scenic splendour for interested parties. Hopefully, some of the images contained herein will inspire somebody to model that particular location but if you're not one of the modelling fraternity then just sit back and enjoy a real journey of nostalgia.

Thanks to the Armstrong Railway Photographic Trust (ARPT) for the loan of many of the images contained herein. Also, many thanks to those photographers who supplied images for inclusion – cheers gentlemen! Finally a mention of the Disused stations website and in particular Alan Young for making life a little easier for this compiler.

David Dunn, Cramlington, May 2017.

(*Cover*) **Newbiggin station in June 1956 with ex-works, and newly converted, V3 No.67651 at the head of a working to Manors. This image allows us to see how the station running-in name-board letters were fixed to the board in a raised fashion with two or more spacers to each letter.** *Stephen Lewins collection.*

(*Previous page*) **Propelling its three-coach push-and-pull set, G5 No.67323 departs Monkseaton station for the carriage siding on 4th June 1958. Once safely across the main line, and when a gap appears between the electric services, the 0-4-4T would bring its train into this platform ready for a service to Blyth.** *I.S.Carr (ARPT).*

Printed and bound by The Amadeus Press, Cleckheaton, West Yorkshire
First published in the United Kingdom by Book Law Publications, 382 Carlton Hill, Nottingham, NG4 1JA

ALSTON BRANCH

Standing in for an absent diesel multiple unit, Blaydon J39 No.64849 is in charge of the Alston branch train at Haltwhistle circa winter 1959/60. Note the make-up of the branch train which consists of a Gresley vehicle and a BR Mk.1 brake. A steam-hauled five-coach Newcastle-Carlisle working has called at the Down platform; diesel multiple units would soon be taking over those workings too but this one could be hauled by a Gresley A3 which were no strangers to this station. Opened throughout by the Newcastle & Carlisle Railway in 1852, the thirteen-mile long Haltwhistle-Alston branch managed to see its centenary, and beyond; though listed for closure by Beeching it survived that massacre only to be crushed eventually by bureaucrats and politicians. Its ideal situation was simply to be there in times of adverse weather, but in the meantime manage on the morsels of passenger usage from a decreasing local population in times of increasing public expenditure, inflation and even greater demands on the public purse. It was never going to survive, except in an ideal world! *W.R.E.Lewis (ARPT)*.

WD No.78588 (90384) runs west through Haltwhistle light-engine in July 1947 after refurbishment at the Scotswood works of Armstrong Whitworth. The 2-8-0 was on test from Blaydon shed and would be allocated to March shed in Cambridgeshire on the following 28th August. How far west the WDs ran during these initial tests is unknown but the locomotive certainly has a nice head of steam. The 2-8-0 never did come back to the north-east, spending its working life on the Eastern Region of BR; it was withdrawn on 26th February 1966. Now then, '...change for Alston' the sign informs intending passengers, however, in later years, under BR ownership, the message on the sign was altered to 'Haltwhistle change for Newcastle & Carlisle'. Note the three adverts on the end of the platform building: Phensic – will stop your pain; Bovril for real beef flavour; Brylcreem! (*A little dab ill do ya*). *Fleetwood Shawe (ARPT).*

Almost ten years later, BR Standard Cl.3 No.77014 waits in the bay platform at Haltwhistle with a midday service to Alston circa 1957. The 2-6-0 had joined sister No.77011 at Blaydon in June 1956 and from June 1955 – when 77011 had transferred to Blaydon from West Auckland – until September 1959 the Standards had worked the Alston branch almost continuously until the introduction and full time use of two-car diesel multiple units during that September. No.77011 had been allocated from Blaydon to Alston sub-shed in December 1955, a cushy number for any locomotive although winters could be tricky. Although the motive power is pure BR, the rolling stock remains LNER with two Gresley vehicles and what looks like a Thompson coach bringing up the rear. Note the adverts adorning the end of the platform building now: Snowcem; and good ol' Brylcreem. The three railwaymen conversing on the platform were fully aware of the signal post and its mechanism but unsuspecting passengers, and especially children may not have realised just what the movements of the lever and chains were, or even that they moved regularly. The River South Tyne meanders past the railway junction, its presence often threatening. *I.S.Carr (ARPT).*

During the afternoon of Saturday 12th April 1952 G5 No.67315 heads the Alston train at Haltwhistle with crew and one other footplateman (Alan Robinson) posing alongside. The 0-4-4T is immaculately turned-out which one might normally put down to a recent visit to main works for a heavy overhaul and repaint. However, this G5 had recently attended Darlington works but only for a Light Intermediate (5th to 22nd March 1952) where repaints and linings were not normally given. The condition of No.67315 is down to its Alston based crew who keep the engine in fine fettle. This G5 had been allocated to Alston since 29th May 1940 and would remain there until reallocated to Blaydon on 7th June 1953; in reality the tank continued working from Alston shed because Blaydon had been its 'official' home since May 1940 when it had transferred from Rothbury after four years there. Again its 'official' allocation was Heaton but that depot out-stationed it to Rothbury. Note the attractive lines of the signal box with its narrow brick-built base and fluted upper works constructed of timber and cast iron. *J.W.Armstrong (ARPT).*

Earlier that day the same three gentlemen pose for J.W.Armstrong whilst standing on the running board of the G5 which is standing on the engine pit adjacent to the turntable at Haltwhistle. This was the means of turning the Alston line motive power and eradicated the need for push-pull workings along with dedicated locomotives and passenger stock. The turntable was located on the south side of the main line just west of the station; the overbridge abutment can be seen on the left; the LNER NE Area Locomotive Shed Diagram book described the facility as being located in Haltwhistle station yard with a 46ft 4in. diameter open-pit, hand-operated turntable, 30ft 0in. long outside engine pit, with an 8in. standard water column (just out of frame to the right). *J.W.Armstrong* (*ARPT*).

Of course we must not forget that Haltwhistle was actually nearer to the Carlisle than it was to Newcastle and it was inevitable that freight would originate at the west end of the line just as much as it did at the east end of the line. Indeed up to 1963 some three freights a week were originating in Carlisle for the Alston branch. On the morning of Saturday 4th April 1959, Carlisle Canal based N2 No.69564 was busy shunting the goods yard alongside the river at Haltwhistle and is recorded during one of those shunting movements which required some thought before the end result was achieved; after this the N2 worked goods up to Alston. How often Canal shed sent the six-coupled tank on this job is unknown but some certainties have come to light: No.69564 was transferred to Carlisle on 26th August 1957 from Parkhead; No.69564 would never wear the second BR crest; the N2's last heavy overhaul was completed at Cowlairs in December 1956, so its external condition is a credit to 12C (the current code for Canal shed); No.69564 was the only N2 allocated to Canal shed during the BR period – four others had been allocated during different periods of LNER days; the 0-6-2T was condemned 20th June 1961. *Howard Forster.*

Crossing the bridge spanning the River South Tyne, J39 No.64853 departs from Haltwhistle with the Alston branch train on 22nd June 1957. The viaduct is substantially but gracefully constructed to accommodate two tracks, with four skew arches over the river section, another at the northern end, and a straight arch on the south bank; triangular buttresses assists the flowing water around the piers to prevent scour. Nowadays, the viaduct is Grade II Listed. The photographer is standing on the flood plain; the surrounding hills on the route up to Alston provide a bountiful supply of water from a vast catchment area. It is worth keeping an eye on the passenger vehicles used on this branch in BR times; here we have nice mixed trio of various origin. *R.H. Leslie, P.J. Robinson collection.*

BR Cl.3 No.77014 gets ready to feel the strain of the forthcoming climb and digs in shortly after leaving the Listed structure, it is already at 1 in 80 but the next mile and a half will be at 1 in 70! Up to 1932 early morning workmen's trains would have stopped at Plenmeller Halt, a private platform established near here in 1919 to serve a nearby colliery but like many things in this area associated with mining, coal or lead, it didn't last long. The d.m.us were still some months off from enticing passengers back onto the trains so in the meantime this Gresley/BR Mk.1 combination on 16th May 1959 will suffice. *R.H. Leslie, P.J. Robinson collection.*

Next stop up the line is Coanwood. This is the new order from 1959: Metro-Camm Class 101 two-car diesel multiple units made something of an impression on the intending public and passenger receipts for the line rose with the enthusiasm. On the last day of September 1961 a young mother with four youngsters make their way to the exit after their trip from Alston. The old timber booking hall building complete with passenger amenities has been demolished and a newly painted fence stands on the threshold of the site whilst a new wooden shed suffices as passenger accommodation. The signal box which dated from the turn-of-the-century has also disappeared but the almost armless post – read onwards – stands defiant! *Malcolm Dunnett* (*ARPT*).

13

Coanwood: Population 1927 – 103 souls. 308 miles from London! Looking uphill towards Alston some nine miles to the south (we are at about 600 feet here); this one mile section of 1 in 525 through Coanwood is probably the easiest part of the route. Beyond the signal box and level crossing is a small goods platform on the left which was complete with a one-ton capacity hand crane – just visible. The line to Coanwood Colliery was located approximately level with the buffer stops of the goods yard; whenever it was taken out, there is no sign of the connection being visible on this date. The colliery itself was situated immediately behind the trees on the left and had been worked since the late 1700s. Besides coal extraction, ovens were on site to produce coke and it was that particular activity which saw the complex close in 1919, the last coal being wound in 1917. Note the (four-and-a) quarter mile post at the end of the timber section of the platform.

14   *Fleetwood Shawe* (*ARPT*).

The public road side of the signal box, and its adjacent wooden hut; note the ramp and platform which was probably a means of getting milk churns on/off carts ready for carriage by rail (we are on the west side of the Pennines and probably low enough here for some dairy farming). The station name board on the ground at the rear of the shed is of LNER origin and had been removed by BR. Coanwood became unstaffed in 1955 and these images probably stem from that period when it was all 'going to the dogs'; although worse was yet to come! *Fleetwood Shawe* (*ARPT*).

Coanwood station was built on the east side of the line and here the timber-built structure with its LNER adornments and notice boards appears in good condition. A 308 yard long passing loop was provided and would have formed the Up line if the branch had prospered into main line status. Though undated, this image was probably recorded during a summer of the late 1930s! The signal box dates from about 1904, the hipped roof design being pure NER; an earlier box stood at the northern end of the platform. The shape of the trees gives a clue as to the direction of the seemingly endless westerly winds. Note the workman leaning against the signal box, awaiting the next train to Alston? *Fleetwood Shawe (ARPT).*

(*opposite*) Coanwood. As seen from the crossing at the south end of the station a few years after nationalisation. Again the provision for a second track is seen here where a passing loop was provided just beyond the platform track. Note that the crossing gates fitted now are of lightweight tubular steel which are chained and pad-locked; the earlier gates visible in the illustration opposite were of heavy timber construction with z frames and a large square-sectioned hinged pole. The roadway on the crossing is not metalled and is simply a dirt track. The station does look dilapidated although it is still open for business. Built in 1877, it replaced a temporary station which was named Shaft Hill and which dated from 1853. The Coanwood moniker was adopted in 1885 and probably echoed the name of an adjacent colliery. Besides the coal mine, a limestone quarry was also located nearby; both industries being rail served. Those two enterprises closed before Grouping but another nearby coal mine, East Coanwood Colliery, which was connected by a tramway, was productive up to about 1938. The eagle-eyed would have noted that the top signal arm (the home) had been removed. Meanwhile, the photographers' motor vehicle is parked at the top of the lane on the right and beyond that are a row of houses known as Herdley Low Terrace, High Terrace was behind those. *Fleetwood Shawe (ARPT).*

Lambley viaduct; probably the most impressive structure on the whole line! Unlike the rest of the branch, this viaduct was built to accommodate a single line of railway. It is perhaps that fact which made it so spectacular although it was 1959, with the introduction of d.m.us, before the public was given the chance to view the now Grade II Listed structure from the front, and rear diesel units. Constructed of dressed and rough-cut stone and 110ft high, the viaduct spans the fairly infant River South Tyne on eighteen arches, nine of which have 58ft spans, the others were two at 12ft and seven at 20ft. This undated autumnal view looks north–east towards the wooded hillside of the gorge. It will be noted that a wooden pedestrian bridge spans the river alongside the viaduct. *Fleetwood Shawe (ARPT).*

(*opposite*) Lambley station, Lambley viaduct – with all nine of the major arches just visible – and the line down to Lambley Colliery! Again this image is undated but we can gain a reasonable idea that the date is pre–1958 because the line to the colliery is still operational. There are no trains in the frame but people are walking the station platform as a Down train is 'pegged'. It was because of the delay in completing the viaduct that the line did not open throughout for passenger traffic until 17th November 1852. From this point to Alston – just under nine miles – goods and mineral traffic had been carried from the previous January; the Haltwhistle-Shafthill section had opened in March 1851 for goods, and 19th July 1851 for passenger traffic. *J.W.Armstrong (ARPT).*

Lambley station circa 1938; the population hereabouts in 1927 was 514 souls. We are 308 miles from London and nearly five miles from Haltwhistle. This vicinity could be a branch line modellers' dream. We have stone, brick, timber and slate all in use for building materials: station, signal box, junction, major branch, minor branch to a coal mine with all the associated assets of a working colliery including an engine shed; not forgetting a platform which couldn't, it seems, make its mind up as to what height it should be. The viaduct is a major feature of the model (at 4mm scale it is just shy of 18ins. or 440mm tall) but the coal branch has an overbridge across its cutting just beyond the siding visible here (probably too far in prototypical scale but we can adjust such things). You could model NER, LNER or BR periods. You could run a two or three coach passenger service with medium and large tank engines; a goods service with six-coupled tender engines and or tank engines; not forgetting the BR Standards and the all-important d.m.us and rail-buses! A list of steam locomotives allocated to Alston shed over the years will be included later besides, think about all those engines which were used but not actually allocated. Now just look at all those timber building which have been finished in a two-tone paint scheme; and who said velox-style windows were a modern idea? The wind-swept trees are readily available commercially so there is a good start. The hill-side location gives any easy finish to the backdrop. I expect to see a surge in the sales of certain models very soon! *Fleetwood Shawe (ARPT).*

(*opposite*) Lambley in BR days! Of course you modellers had better make your mind up because the period either side of Nationalisation appear to be real opposites as regards the external condition of everything. Unkempt and dilapidation rules-the-roost here and the colliery branch appears to be derelict with stored wagons in place. Of course the branch to the colliery was entitled the Brampton Railway and of which more in Volume 2. Strangely Lambley station employed staff until 1966. The station site is another section of the route where it was difficult to locate a second track, the station's situation on the hill side proving rather tight! The gradient just here is about 1 in 198 but it soon steepens to 1 in 112 and then 1 in 100. *Fleetwood Shawe (ARPT).*

Looking south-east along the colliery branch (Brampton Railway) towards Lambley junction and the passenger station; the date is probably circa 1956 with everything appearing pristine and maintained – track bed excepted! Lambley Colliery which was located less than half a mile behind the photographer where this branch line had turned through 90 degrees onto a south-westerly heading from its present north-westerly alignment. During its later life under the auspices of the National Coal Board from 1947, Lambley Colliery was employing about seventy men lifting from between 14,000 to 28,000 tons of saleable coal a year – 200 to 400 tons per man per year! As already mentioned closure took place in 1958. The mine was basically the last big employer in the area where once there had been dozens of lead and coal mines, limestone quarries and a host of other minerals worked out during the 18th, 19th, and early 20th centuries. Now, is it me or is there a bit of a gradient up to the junction. *Fleetwood Shawe (ARPT)*.

With the colliery branch now lifted, Kingmoor based Ivatt Cl.4 No.43121 works a five-coach enthusiasts special – complete with a kitchen car – along the main branch towards Alston on Monday 27th March 1967 as the finale of a long weekend rail tour – *SCOTTISH RAMBLER* NO.6. Note that a lot of the station's infrastructure is either changed or demolished, including the signals. *Maurice Burns.*

Looking due south through the bridge arch spanning the Lambley Colliery branch at Harper Town, just below Lambley passenger station. Lambley viaduct can be seen too; in the far distance is Ashholme Common at 1,466 feet. Although undated, the seasonal view is probably an autumn afternoon. Note that the rails are well used with all the coal originating at the colliery coming out via this end of the Brampton Railway. *Fleetwood Shawe* (*ARPT*).

A same day view from the bridge illustrated opposite. Yet another aspect of Lambley viaduct, spoilt perhaps – maybe even enhanced – by the rather untidy embankment of the branch line; however, the eagle-eyed will have noted the chickens and ducks mooching and scratching around the abandoned sleepers; accommodation for the fowl is there amongst the wood and metal but it is difficult to distinguish from the rubbish. Note the limestone outcrop towering above the east bank of the river; it was on the other side of the viaduct that the same outcrop of rock provided enough stone to create a quarry employing about fifty men for a couple of years from about 1894. The then followed one of those triangular legal problems whereby the NER stopped the quarrying company from extracting any more stone because it might undermine the railway. The quarry company demanded compensation but then so did the landowner who had both parties at his mercy. A figure was eventually agreed with the quarry operators but the landowner wanted more so it was back to years of negotiation where greed appeared to win. The Whinstone Company lost out altogether and ceased operations before 1914. As usual in such long drawn out disputes the solicitors were the real winners. Of course the NER also lost a valuable customer on a stretch of railway where the various business interests were folding at an alarming rate. *Fleetwood Shawe (ARPT).*

Somewhere north of Slaggyford in 1951, Blaydon J39 No.64812 has charge of what appears to be an afternoon excursion from a mystery origin consisting six BR Mk.1 coaches; we can only guess as to the destination but my money is on Alston! Note the rather nicely turned-out 0-6-0; I wonder what this particular working was really about. Was it market day? *E.E.Smith, M. Halbert collection.*

Slaggyford station – Saturday 27th October 1956 – with not a soul in sight! Laid out to double-track proportions, the semi-redundant line was acting as a run-round, and goods siding, for the loading bank on the right at the north end. The station house stood to the right – off frame – near the goods store. Seen from the level crossing, the platform building comprised the booking office and two waiting rooms; the timber-built structure was brought into use in 1890 whilst the substantial signal box dates from a later period but is North Eastern in origin. Slaggyford was located in the middle of a one and a half mile stretch on 1 in 155 – not exactly easy but not exactly hard either. *L.Turnbull* (*ARPT*).

Slaggyford in LNER days; it may, perhaps, be winter, and damp, but the place looks inviting enough. The name board is painted in the sans serif style adopted by the LNER under the font name Gill Sans. The advertisements are plugging destinations served by the LNER: Carlisle; Durham; York. The war is threatening somewhere in Europe but if it had gotten this far, shattering this idyll, we would have lost already! *Fleetwood Shawe* (*ARPT*).

Slaggyford, 31st October 1964. Population 1927 – ? Distance from London 312 miles, distance from village was a quarter mile, and west thereof. The seed of doubt has been sown by Dr.Beeching but for once road transport inadvertently came to the rescue of the railways because the branch was reprieved – for the time-being – the local road system being deemed inadequate for the purpose of winter motoring. The platform has been shortened (it's funny how the edges have to be removed as if to prove a point) prior to the erection of a wooden barrier – a fence to match the original – inhibiting passengers from progressing further down the platform. It is now long enough for a two-car d.m.u. All we need now is a new name board in BR corporate upper and lower case finish; the LNER example is looking rather tired. Meanwhile, Slaggyford looks a mess. The station house is visible on the left, as is the level crossing with the original gates still working but for how long? Note the young boy stood to the left of the crossing with a full grown goat next to him! The coal drops or cells were to the immediate left and slightly behind the cameraman. *C.J.B.Sanderson* (*ARPT*).

More detail for the modeller! Slaggyford coal cells on a quiet day. This is post rather than pre-war; the dilapidation inherited by BR is plain to see even though this installation has been kept fairly tidy. *Fleetwood Shawe (ARPT).*

Alston, Cumberland, population 1927 – ? Miles from London 317; population 1950 – 2,600; 2017 – 1,128! What went wrong? In 1831 – the peak of industrial (mining) activity in the area – the population of the Alston Moor parish was 6,858 souls, today (2011 figures) it is down to just 2,088 including the town's population but still it is falling. Whatever the 1927 population was, it was probably falling because of all the mining closures during the early years of the century, and beforehand. The railway it may be said, was a little late in getting to this once thriving but somewhat isolated mining area which probably saw its most productive period just when the line was authorised in the 1840s. In 2005 the town of Alston had something of an imbalance regarding the population whereby there were apparently ten males for every female! Pleas were sent out and even a TV programme was made to highlight the problem but it is still rather one-sided up there!! Situated at 1,000 feet above sea level, Alston shares – with Buxton, Derbyshire – the title of 'highest market town in England'. The way things are going, that title could well become 'the highest ghost town...' shades of certain towns in Nevada, Colorado, and other faraway isolated ex-mining communes! This general view of the station – circa 1938 – shows one of the branch engines – J21 No.51 – being coaled, its tender groaning under the load already stacked. It is interesting to see that the station yard is also the forecourt, there being no segregation between passengers and goods. The United bus may well be the service to Carlisle which would have worked over to Brampton from here to join with the A69 trunk road. It is summer time but the town is strangely quiet! *Fleetwood Shawe (ARPT)*.

31

Alston goods on 12th September 1950 with coal hoppers on the cells to the right, barrels stacked on the goods landing, a stone (what else) built goods shed, the signal box, and that massive snowplough which had just arrived for the winter season requirements. A snowplough had been stationed at Alston since at least 1888 when a newly-built NER six-wheel vehicle weighing 22½ tons was positioned here. From 1895 it was numbered 82506 in the wagon fleet series but from 1908 it became No.4 in the NER series dedicated to the snowploughs. From the earliest days it was given accommodation in its own shed at Alston and it was for this reason that a stove was not installed as was normally the case with other ploughs on the NER. No.4 remained at Alston to at least 1935 but by 1947 – probably when the shed went – it had been replaced by No.14 a 26-ton model dating from 1901 and latterly stationed at Waskerley. It is that particular plough illustrated here and by now numbered 900568 in the LNER Departmental series (this plough did have heating and a cooking stove). After this image was recorded, another similar plough took its place in 1954; the old No.13, also of 1901 vintage but having an open veranda and somewhat lighter at twenty and a bit tons; it was numbered 900567. No.900567 left Alston when the shed closed in 1959 and was taken to Gateshead initially but what happened to it thereafter is a mystery. *L.G.Charlton.*

The Alston station house and yard, Tuesday 12th September 1950; again the public and industrial space comes together with no actual conflict taking place. A Chevrolet – I stand to be corrected – tipper lorry waits on the approach road perhaps with a view to picking up some item; the vehicle was possibly a recent relic from wartime which was purchased 'for a song' at an army surplus sale by some enterprising local entrepreneur. On the extreme right can be seen the jib of the Goods Department 3-ton crane, hand powered, it could nevertheless do the necessary. Two rivers – the Nent and the South Tyne – join here, just north of the station. The former flows in from the east whilst the Tyne continues its relentless course from the south. Overlooking proceedings at Alston is Park Fell (1676ft) which was just one of many Pennine high points on that great land mass which was then mainly in Cumberland. From here we get a good view of the roof over the station's only platform. The roof, and that on the engine shed were taken down in the mid-1960s as a prelude to closure but mainly to get around the problem of having to maintain it after years of neglect. *L.G.Charlton.*

Standing at the centre of the goods operation at Alston was the goods shed, a rather magnificent edifice constructed to receive, sort, and despatch all manner of goods from the market town and its catchment area. A substantial structure employing buttresses on each corner of the building, and with adequate facility for wagons and carts; the goods office would hopefully have been doing lots of work but over the years the demand on the railway's goods services was receding annually so that by 1965 the service was withdrawn from the whole line. It is still September 1950 and what looks like that Chevrolet lorry depicted on the previous page is now down in the yard. As an aside, a similar Chevrolet tipper was observed working at a paper mill in Greenfield near Oldham in the 1980s. Well worn, it was neither taxed, plated, or probably not even registered; it travelled only about a mile on each of its two daily trips over private roads shifting waste from the paper making process up to a private tip in a valley such as this one; longevity indeed! Note that the wagons on the coal cells have been changed but otherwise activity is minimal. *Fleetwood Shawe (ARPT).*

A final look at the goods yard with its now wagon-less coal cells (note that both six-bar gates have been closed, perhaps its weekend?); the cells were built with the station in 1851. The grounded van body in the centre foreground must have been in use as a store of sorts, typical recycling of the period where withdrawn vehicles could find further life as, chicken coups, pig sheds, tool stores, and cricket pavilions for up and coming clubs! The hut on the left was part of a range of buildings used for coal offices and a weighbridge. Again an unknown date but it must be summer because the foliage is thick on the trees and the showers keeps coming and going. Modellers note the two different buffer types employed on the coal cells indicating perhaps some vigorous shunting in the past took out one of the original sets. The photographer is using the vantage point of a bridge on the Hexham road, the siding in the foreground ran beneath the road to the premises of the Alston Lime & Coal Company but in the latter BR period the siding was defunct and used for wagon storage. *Fleetwood Shawe* (*ARPT*).

The terminal end of Alston station with the G5 No.67315 on an afternoon arrival from Haltwhistle, 12th April 1952. The turntable here, which dated from 1868, had been condemned shortly after Nationalisation. Resident J39 No.64851 pokes out of the shed, its work for the day completed it seems? The original plans for the line, as authorised 26th August 1846, depicted the terminus at Nenthead some three miles further south and east than Alston. Tickets issued at this station at this time amounted to just over 6,000 annually, a half of the amount issued forty years previously. During most of the BR period with steam in charge, there were five return passenger trains a day from Alston but on Saturdays this was increased to seven. Various geographical surveys put the station at 905ft. above sea level which puts the church in the background at a steady one thousand feet a.s.l! *J.W.Armstrong (ARPT).*

By the time BR came into being, Alston engine shed could boast to having two locomotives in use daily and to run those, with the aid of four crews, all stationed at Alston. During this time, and in practice it was something which had gone on for years, there was a daily goods from Alston which left around midday but the colliery at Lambley would sometimes require servicing too; in which case the goods engine would leave Alston as pilot to the first northbound passenger working, detach at Lambley, take full mineral wagons down to Haltwhistle, return empties to the colliery, and await a late morning passenger working for Alston. This undated image shows Blaydon J39 No.64849 is in charge of the passenger working. Not exhaustive, this is the known Alston shed allocations over the years from Grouping – figures in brackets are the LNER numbers, where none exist LNER numbers are presented: F8: 35 – 1/1/23-0/12/24; 172 – 0/12/24-7/9/25; 1599 – 14/2/24-0/12/24; G5: 67247 (1788) – 1/5/33-17/1/36; 67251 (1838) – 7/9/25-19/9/30; 67259 (1795) – 27/5/40-2/6/41; 67277 (405) – 15/5/42-18/1/43; 67305 (1755) – 29/5/40-5/5/41; 67315 (2086) – 29/5/40-7/6/53; 67326 (2097) – by 6/12/23-0/7/24; J21: (51) – 17/1/36-28/3/43; 65100 (1122) – 18/1/43-28/11/48; J25: 65718 (2131) – 0/12/25-8/9/30; J39: 64812 (1418) – 4/1/53-7/6/53; 64816 (1470) – 20/7/51-3/9/51 (on loan from Blaydon whilst 64851 in works); 64851 (1468) – 2/1/49-4/1/53; N8: 9380 (863) – 19/9/30-1/5/33; Y1: 68141 (106) – 29/3/41-15/5/42. Ivatt Cl.4 Nos.43126 – 5/53-3/54; 43128 – 5/53-5/55; the last of them, chronologically, was BR Standard Cl.3 No.77011 – 12/55-9/59. Notes: F8 No.35 was already resident at Grouping. The Sentinel was used for 'extra' shunting during its period of residency as additional stone traffic for war materials were being handled; it was transferred to Gateshead, replaced by G5 No.405. Perhaps the strangest locomotives allocated to Alston were two D49 Nos.62737 (211) THE YORK AND AINSTY – 27/5/40-2/11/40; 62765 (362) THE GOATHLAND – 29/5/40-2/11/40; along with a C7 Atlantic No.2996 (2211) – 29/5/40-2/11/40. Neither of the three actually worked the branch and were simply 'hiding' up at Alston as a wartime expedient. Realising the assets were of no use stored in the hills, the authorities transferred them back to work; the D49s to Tweedmouth whereas the C7 went to Gateshead. And so ended a six-month episode of 'namers' being allocated to Alston sub-shed. Three G5s also came with the tender engines at the same time (27-29/5/40) and they are included in the list under G5; it is not known if they too were exempt duties! More to the point, where did they keep them all? *K.H.Cockerill (ARPT)*. 37

Alston engine shed closed 27th September 1959 and diesel multiple units took over the passenger workings from Haltwhistle. From that date onwards the first train of the day started from Haltwhistle at 0630; it ran non-stop to Alston to form the 0705 all stations to Haltwhistle. From 2nd November the weekday frequency of trains became six return journeys whilst Saturdays remained unchanged at seven. This was an improvement from the final steam services which comprised four trains each way (SX) with three extras on Saturdays. With a determination normally lacking within BR in such circumstances, it was reported that they wanted to make the branch pay to the point of no longer issuing Cheap Day return tickets (at 2/10d [14p]) for the thirteen mile journey, and instead were making passengers pay an increase to the ordinary Second Class return from 4/9d. to 5/10d! Of course, there was no alternative direct bus service between the two centres so BR really was 'screwing the locals.' And you thought the latter situation was a modern TOC affair. *Fleetwood Shawe (ARPT)*.

Autumn at Haltwhistle! As a two-car Metro-Camm unit departs for Alston on Saturday 14th October 1961. In the background are two bridges spanning the South Tyne which has plenty of space to expand during the coming winter months; the furthest of the bridges is the viaduct carrying the Alston branch and illustrated to better effect on pages 9 & 10. On 28th August 1963 it was reported that trains were quite well patronised on this day. Repairs were to begin on Hambley viaduct and it is possible that a short length of track would be re-laid down the mineral line near the viaduct to accommodate wagons. The steam hauled freight from Carlisle normally made three trips a week to Alston, though all the lead and lime traffic has now ceased; coal is the main mineral traffic for the stations on the branch still able to handle it. Ten years later on Tuesday 17th July 1973 an Immingham based Class 47 No.1622 paid a visit to the branch with an inspection saloon; that event was apparently a first for the class and the branch. It was reported in early 1975 that traffic on the Newcastle-Carlisle line was increasing so fast that it was apparently described as Britain's fastest developing line! Passenger and freight carryings were up and new signalling had helped the improvements. Even the threatened Alston branch had shown an increase in passengers! However, a year later and another somewhat alarming but not unexpected report stated that '...the Haltwhistle-Alston branch was expected to close 2nd May 1976.' The line closed officially on Monday (like they all did it seems) 3rd May 1976! *Malcolm Dunnett* (*ARPT*).

There have been no major accidents on the branch during its lifetime but a notable incident with no injury or loss of life is worth recalling: When an engine over-nighting on Alston shed gradually lost steam pressure it then released its steam brake – no hand brake having been applied – and covertly chuffed off into the dark with the remaining head of steam giving it some momentum after which gravity took over. When the crew arrived in the morning their steed was nowhere to be seen and upon investigation they apparently found it upright but in the river (I'm not sure which part of the river), a set of catch points doing what they were installed for! This undated image shows J39 No.4921 and another of the class with the Gateshead and Darlington breakdown cranes attending an unknown incident on the line but at what location. Is it the county line between Cumberland and Northumberland? Note that both cranes have their jibs raised almost to the maximum height which also equates to the maximum lift, normally. Both appliances have stabilising beams employed so whatever it was they were rescuing must have been in that piece of ground between and in front of them? To pinpoint the dates more precisely, the 0-6-0 was renumbered 4921 on 16th June 1946, ex-1544, and then became No.64921 from 23rd April 1948. Well done those of you who spotted another plume of smoke to the north, behind this entourage. It looks as though the cranes are about to retrieve something which is down the bank on the right! *Fleetwood Shawe (ARPT).*

THE AMBLE BRANCH

A 5¾ mile railway was opened from Chevington Wood on the ECML in September 1849 by the York, Newcastle & Berwick Railway. Except for a couple of minor cuttings and one embankment, there were no major earthworks on the branch. Initially the line was operated as freight only but passenger services began 1878. There were two stations on the line, Broomhill serving the mining community there and the terminus at Amble; both built in 1878. Chevington, regarded as the junction station for the line, was located just over a mile south of where the branch joined the main line. In one of those quirks which a fairly rare in British railway operating practice, the line was single from the ECML junction to just east of Broomhill station but from there to Amble it was double! This is the view on 26th April 1952 looking east towards the double track section from the A1068 road bridge. *J.W.Armstrong (ARPT).*

(*above*) Amble passenger station on 26th April 1952 virtually intact some twenty-two years after closure to passengers; the parachute water tank has disappeared so too have the advertisements. Coal was still big business and the sidings here were convenient for the staiths located further east. J.W.Armstrong (ARPT). (*below*) The actual staiths at Amble overlooking a stretch of water known as Warkworth Harbour although Warkworth (population 1927 – 1,042 souls, and one mile from its railway station, which is 303 miles from London) is situated a mile upstream from this location. The date is 24th June 1966 and the installation was still in business but not on this Friday without a ship alongside. This industrial gem was dismantled and had disappeared by 1972 bringing an end to deep mining in this part of Northumberland. *L.G.Charlton.*

Passenger services, which had been running five trains each-way on weekdays, and eight on Saturdays with a late night service from Amble to Broomhill only, ceased in July 1930 following a sharp decline in patronage during the 1920s when motor bus services began; an F8 provided by Alnmouth shed worked the branch daily. This is No.1160 with a typical two-coach make-up in 1930, on what must have been one of the final workings. Alnmouth had two F8s for the Amble branch duty. No.1160 had been resident before Grouping and remained loyal to the shed until condemned on 19th January 1934. The other was No.485 which had also been resident prior to 1st January 1923. It was transferred to Tweedmouth on 14th July 1930, a week after the cessation of the passenger services on the Amble branch. Whenever operational requirements dictated, Tweedmouth shed would provide cover for either of the Alnmouth F8s. Goods engines were not given the same treatment as the passenger locomotives and they just worked onto the branch whenever required which was normally every day. A lot of the shunting was carried out by the NCB's own locomotives. The smallest of the north-east harbours used for the export of coal, Amble is a seaport, and a civil parish located at the mouth of River Coquet. Full name: Amble-by-the-Sea. Population in 2011 was 6,025 souls in 1927 it had been 4,851. Amble gained the moniker 'Friendliest Port' in the 1930s when the RMS Mauretania (1906-1934), which was passing, and in sight of the shore whilst heading to the breakers at Rosyth in July 1935, the town council at Amble sent a telegram stating "Still the finest ship on the seas". The ship replied with the greeting "To the last and kindliest port in England." En route from Southampton to Scotland, the popular liner had called in on the Tyne, her birthplace, for a final farewell and where the Lord Mayor of Newcastle boarded her. *Alf York collection.*

North Blyth based J27 No.65792 shunts coal wagons on the double track section of the branch between Broomhill and Amble in April 1952. Mining interests near here included the rail connected collieries at Broomhill (employed 1,600 producing 280,000 tons plus p.a., closed 1961 when production combined with Hauxley); Hauxley (opened in 1927 and employed 336 men in 1947 producing 165,000 tons plus p.a. Closed 1966); Radcliffe situated between those two mines, had closed prior to Vesting Day in 1947. Closure of the branch to general goods was in May 1964 at Broomhill and December at Amble. Coal traffic, on and off the branch continued until 6th October 1969. The highest annual tonnage on the branch was during the 1920s when 750,000 p.a. was being carried. *J.W.Armstrong (ARPT).*

(*opposite, top*) Over the long-weekend of Friday 27th September to Tuesday 1st October 1963, the RCTS and SLS organised a joint North Eastern Rail Tour which took in numerous lines in the Region. On Sunday 29th, Amble was one of the destinations and here in the near empty yard of the erstwhile Amble passenger station during the late afternoon, Ivatt Cl.4 No.43057 runs round its train prior to working it back to the ECML and then on to the Wansbeck line. *I.S.Carr (ARPT).* (*opposite*) With admirers young and old looking on, NCB 0-6-0 side tank No.28 is shunting the staiths at Amble in 1968. *D.R. Dunn collection.*

44

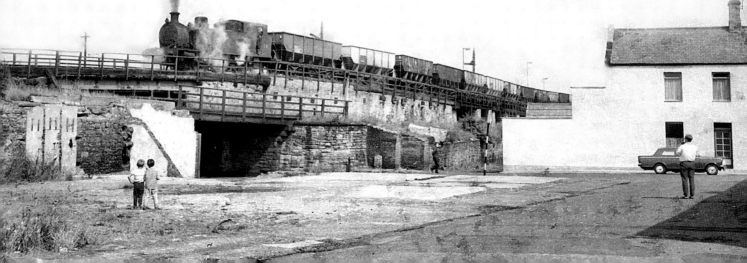

As an electric service departs for Newcastle from the Up platform, G5 No.67281 in the Down platform prepares to propel its three-coach push-pull set into the carriage sidings on the Up side where it will set back into the Up platform to form the next service to Blyth via the Avenue branch. Monkseaton station has been very 'mobile' throughout its life: Starting out as Whitley on 1st April 1861 (there must be a clue in there!?), it was replaced on 27th June 1864. It was then renamed and re-sited in 1882, and in 1915, 25th July to be exact, it was re-sited again on the deviation. To finish off its continuous metamorphous to date, it closed on 10th September 1979 for the Tyne & Wear conversion but re-opened 11th August 1980. During the BR period it was ranked – by tickets issued – as second only to Newcastle (Central) amongst the Coast Circle stations. How much the Blyth trains via the Avenue branch contributed to the total is unknown. The latter branch can be seen through the bridge, deviating off to the right. *I.S.Carr (ARPT).*

The G5 (they were normally South Blyth allocated) wheels the next Blyth service into the Up platform at Monkseaton on that 4th day of June 1958. The whole Blyth service operation at this station had to be handled with efficiency because of the each-way 20-minute interval service run by the electric units. From arrival off the Avenue branch, a slick turn-around was required whereby the G5 and its p&p set had then to cross over the electric lines into the carriage siding, allow an Up electric service to arrive and depart, then reverse – engine first – into the Up platform, pick up the intending passengers for Blyth and set off without delaying any of the electric services. It was all done with a touch of nonchalance by now, the staff and everybody involved knowing the procedure inside out! By summer 1950 the timetable for the B&T system revealed a remarkable lack of services between the morning and evening rush periods. For instance, the last Monkseaton to Blyth train in the morning departed at 0912 and the first train running in the opposite direction from Blyth was at 1640. Saturdays were somewhat better to cater for shopping and other non-occupational activities. Monkseaton became the centre of operations from January 1955 to cut operating costs whilst improving connections to the north Tyne suburban coastal stations. June 1958 saw the introduction of diesel multiple units and on Saturdays a regular interval hourly service was introduced between Monkseaton and Blyth. These connected with Newbiggin–Manors trains at Newsham. *I.S.Carr (ARPT)*.

47

And now for a little horticultural interlude: It became a tradition in numerous areas of BR whereby stations would cultivate a garden to competition standards and an annual contest was staged with inspections followed by prizes for winning displays. The North Eastern Region of BR had something of a green-streak running through its personnel already if pre-war activities are anything to go by and gardening was second-nature to most of them. Monkseaton's staff were not to be left out of any such deviation from the normal working day so they created this little display at the south end of the Down platform which was being judged by two knowledgeable gentlemen on an unknown summer afternoon in the 1950s. It is another unknown how Monkseaton faired in the judging; perhaps out there someone would have the results from all those summers ago. Note the advertisements – there must be a clue there too!? *M.Halbert collection.*

(*opposite, left*) A Blyth service with No.67281 in charge enters the Avenue branch at Monkseaton on 3rd June 1958. *I.S.Carr. (ARPT).*
(*opposite, right*) The tablet exchange platform at Monkseaton in September 1957, with G5 No.67261 heading onto the Avenue branch with a Blyth train. *Christopher Campbell.*

Standards were slipping! A rather dirty G5 No.67323 departs from Monkseaton on a crisp Saturday 11th January 1958. This engine was no stranger to these services, but it didn't have much longer to work them with the diesel units waiting in the wings for their turn. When the d.m.us did arrive, South Blyth shed put this 0-4-4T into storage and that's where it remained until condemned on 8th December 1958. The improvements brought about by the introduction of diesel services did not bring the desired and expected huge increase in passenger traffic or revenues as it had done in other parts of the country. More to the point, Beeching had seen the results of four years of diesel services and had included the B&T stations in his report for the mass closures. Blyth with its 40,000 population and Ashington with its 30,000 became two of the largest towns in Britain to lose their passenger services. The last trains ran on Saturday 30th October 1964. *Christopher Campbell.*

(*above and below*) When the Queen came to visit Tyneside on 29th October 1954 the Royal train spent the night on the Avenue branch with V3s 67689 (of Gateshead) and 67653 (of Blaydon) as motive power. Both had recently received General overhauls, which is no surprise! These two images show the slight curve near Crow Hill, and the line near Seaton. About a third of the way from Monkseaton to Hartley a junction veered off in a north-easterly direction to the coast at Seaton Sluice, it had an intermediate station at Brierdene and the branch was known as the Collywell Bay line. That particular branch will be covered in Vol.2 of this series. Carrying on in a northerly direction, and covering a similar amount of route, we come to the site of a south facing junction at Dairy House. Between 1851 and 1853 this provided a direct route from Hartley and from Seghill off a spur just south of Hartley station via a waggon-way to Seaton Sluice but its fortunes came and went when the Blyth & Tyne restricted any passenger trains to run on the main line only. Seaton Sluice was one unlucky village as far as railways were concerned. *R.F.Payne & J.G.Dewing, M.Halbert collection.*

Avenue Crossing signal box towards the end of its life and looking rather run down with rainwater gutters missing or broken, even the slotted signal post looks ready for a coat of paint! Manning this box must have been a lonely vigil in early BR days when the train service outside of the rush periods didn't really exist. Perhaps that's what it was all about – unmanned between certain hours during the day. We are looking north-east across the A190 highway on an unknown date. The passenger station known as The Avenue was located just around here; it dated from 1861 when the single line from Hartley to Monkseaton, known as The Avenue branch was opened. The station's operational life was somewhat short at just three years because it closed on 27th June 1864, perhaps with a view to being re-opened at a later date, but it never did re-open and simply passed into history. *Ian Spencer.*

Exchanging the tablet at Hartley signal box! This pre-1958 image shows the fireman of a Blyth-bound train, which was leaving the Avenue branch, exchanging the tablet with the signalman who is standing on the specially provided platform for such events. Just a little beyond the signal box, a set of points (barely discernible below the outstretched arm) will switch this train onto the Down line for the rest of its journey north. *J.W.Armstrong (ARPT)*.

53

In the days when the station at Hartley was fully operational, a Blyth-Monkseaton service departs for the south on a lovely summer evening circa 1956. The porter acknowledges the fireman who was having a break from his lonely duty in the cab of South Blyth based G5 No.67339. Note the gardens and tidiness of the platform; even the other side of the track has some well cared-for and manicured shrubbery – those were the days? *J.W. Armstrong (ARPT).*

(*opposite, top*) The abandoned Avenue branch platform at Hartley on Saturday 13th August (you can tell by the rain) 1966. The bungalow was probably the crossing keeper's residence although his duties would have included doubling-up as a porter and ticket collector too when the line was operational. This particular platform stood for many years after the main line platforms were swept away by demolition.
(*opposite*) A look back at Hartley station from the north on that damp August Saturday in 1966; the Avenue branch had been closed after the last trains ran on 31st October 1964. Hartley station replaced one located slightly to the west named Hartley Pit. It was situated on the north side of the level crossing on the eastern edge of the village and opened in 1851. Besides the sharply curved platforms on the main line to Seghill, it also had this dedicated and slightly curved platform for the Avenue branch. Closed officially to passengers on Monday 2nd November 1964, the goods facility had been withdrawn from 9th December 1963. That signal box was a 1960 addition replacing the original (*as seen on page 53*) on the east side of the Up line. We'll visit Hartley again in Vol.3. Both *C.J.B.Sanderson (ARPT).*

CHATHILL-SEAHOUSES BRANCH - North Sunderland Railway

Chathill for Seahouses station with Y7 No.68089 in the North Sunderland Railway bay and a V2 running into the Down platform with a stopping passenger train circa 1950; it must have been summer time because the hole in the rear of the cab sheet of the Y7 had a board placed into it during the cooler months of the year. This station predates the NSR by some fifty-one years and, it is still in existence though slightly different now from this illustration. Back to the NSR side of the station and note the driver staring contentedly at the cameraman. The railway crossed three water courses and traversed six cuttings, three level crossings, and two overbridges. Four miles and six chains long, passenger trains normally took twenty minutes for the journey from Chathill to Seahouses. The Depression years of the 1920s and 30s' hit the NSR hard and in 1939 the LNER who became the biggest creditor took the concern over and had the Newcastle District Goods Superintendent administer the running of the railway. It was not what the company had envisioned in 1892 when the railway was authorised. *W.A.Camwell, M.Halbert collection.*

The passenger station at North Sunderland, long after its 29th October 1951 closure! The building was apparently used by a Scout group at this time but it has since fallen down. Opened with the line in December 1898, the less than generous accommodation was clad in corrugated iron throughout. It stood on the south side of the line, west of the crossing. An extension was added in 1901 so that the train guard and his wife could reside here; she then took up the duty of Crossing Keeper. Between North Sunderland station and Seahouses station, a junction was planned to connect with an extension to Bamburgh. This was never built nor was a station which was proposed for Fleetham, about a mile from Chathill. We mustn't forget the other idea of creating a holiday resort between Seahouses and Bamburgh – it would have been nice no doubt. Back to the real world, stone from Pasture Hill quarry, located approximately half a mile north of the mid-point of the route, was taken down to the harbour in two converted ex-Highland passenger coaches acting as goods vehicles, the only goods stock the NSR owned! *M.Halbert collection.*

No.68089 at Seahouses in 1951 with vans at either end of the passenger vehicles. It appears that fish was being loaded into the trailing vehicle, an insulated fish van – fish became the mainstay of the lines finances, with no reliance on the meagre passenger revenue. Note the run-round track with its parsimonious use of sleepers. Unlike the Amble branch, coal was never a factor with this railway, it was all about fishing and grand ideas for holiday resorts. The former traffic was never enough to make a difference and the later remained simply dreams as the railway could not pay its creditors never mind embark on big ideas! The only coal carried on the branch was inbound for domestic and residential use and to supply the tiny fishing fleet. *J.W.Armstrong (ARPT).*

58

Even the four-wheel insulated fish vans seemed to tower over the diminutive Y7. This is No.68089 and friends on arrival at Seahouses 19th May 1951. The main line companies provided the rolling stock to carry the fish, and other commodities off the railway to markets far and wide but the NSR provided its own passenger stock: Five passenger vehicles – all 4-wheel and ancient – were initially operated (all ex-Highland Railway G class rib-sided stock) one of which was converted into a brake composite. They retained HR livery but were given NSR numbers, and were modified to use Westinghouse braking. Besides the two vehicles illustrated on page 61, the NSR bought four other coaches as follows: 1911 – NER Dia. 58 4-wheel, 5-compartment number 1980; withdrawn 1938; 1912 – NER Dia. X 4-wheel, 3-compartment unknown number; withdrawn 1934; 1937 – GER 6-wheel, 6-compartment, LNER No.60916, NSR No.2 (from 1943); withdrawn 1951; 1937 – GER 6-wheel, 6-compartment, LNER No.62305; withdrawn 1939. An ex-NER auto-coach was also borrowed but the Diagram and fleet number are unknown. *C.J.B.Sanderson (ARPT).*

The end of the line or to be more precise, the engine shed at Seahouses in 1951 with the Y7 at home. Like most of the other buildings on the NSR it too was clad in corrugated metal sheets but the pitched roof was covered in slates shortly after it was built. Located just beyond the end of the station platform the shed was built with the line; a number of locomotives have been sheltered here over the fifty-odd year life of the NSR. When it was an independent concern the first locomotive to work the line was a Manning Wardle 0-6-0T BAMBURGH built in 1898 and rebuilt in 1920 lasting until 1947. After borrowing an Armstrong Whitworth four-wheel diesel locomotive in 1933 the company decided to purchase one and THE LADY ARMSTRONG was duly put to work until 1946 when it was withdrawn. The NER and LNER had loaned steam locomotives for short periods whenever the MW tank required maintenance and one such event in 1925 saw J79 No.407 hired to the NSR from 7th to 16th October; no doubt the 1920 rebuilding of the MW tank attracted a similar NER engine too. In 1945 Y7 No.986 was on hire and that 0-4-0T remained at the railway until closure, however, that engine had been preceded onto the NSR property by sister No.985 from 18th May 1942; as No.8088 it transferred to London in June 1948 leaving No.8089 in sole charge! Typically, No.8089 required works attention (General overhaul 18th October to 11th November 1948) and an alternative engine had to be found for the short period of absence. Enter former Lancashire & Yorkshire 0-4-0ST No.11217 on 15th September; allocated to Tweedmouth (52D) for the period of the loan, the ex-LMS saddletank returned to Burton-on-Trent on 18th December 1948 after the return of the Y7 as No.68089 from Darlington in November. It was probably some of the hardest work done by the ex-Lanky Pug which usually worked yards rather than doing four-mile, six-chain 'sprints' at the then regulation 15 m.p.h.; reduced from the original 20 m.p.h. because of the state of the track. BRITISH RAILWAYS now adorned the tank sides of the Y7 above its number, a livery situation which was to remain with the tank until it was sold to Harbour & General Works Ltd. in January 1952 still retaining its smokebox numberplate and 52D shed plate and named EVE, to be used on a sewerage contract at Morecambe, Lancashire; that finished in December 1955 and the Y7 was duly scrapped. *J.W.Armstrong (ARPT)*.

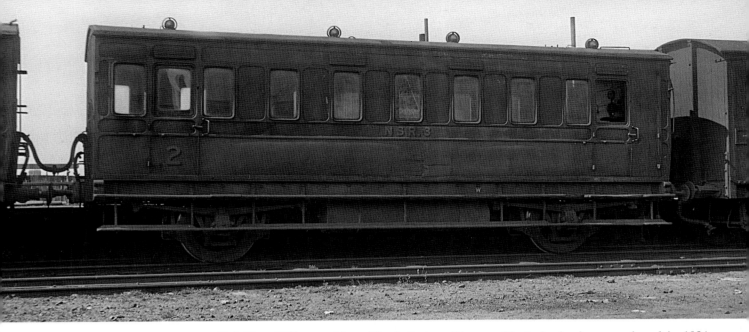

(*above*) Photographed at Seahouses on 19th May 1951, was this ex-North Eastern Diagram 61, 4-wheel saloon purchased in 1924; renumbered NSR No.3 from 1943, it was withdrawn in 1951. (*below*) Recorded on the same day, in the same train at Seahouses, was NSR No.1, a former Great Eastern 6-wheel, 6-compartment vehicle purchased from the LNER in 1937 as their No.60883; renumbered in 1943, it was also withdrawn in 1951. Both *C.J.B.Sanderson* (*ARPT*).

NEWBIGGIN Branch

Newbiggin station throat on an unknown date towards the end of operations; the sidings are becoming weed strewn and little bits of dilapidation are creeping in – the running-in board has lost its top fillet and therefore some of its waterproof integrity – although the asphalt on the platform still appears pristine. The colliery washery (it was actually a dry cleaning plant) on the north side of the line had also seen better days (although it was only commissioned in 1933) and is derelict having closed a few years before its parent Newbiggin Colliery which opened for business in 1910 (sunk in 1908) and eventually employed some 1400 men winding 470,000 tons at its peak in 1940. During the NCB years it was producing between 268,000 and 109,000 tons of saleable coal; the mine ceased production on 11th November 1967. From here to a point adjacent to Woodhorn Colliery just over a mile away, the line was single-track. *Roy Stevens.*

(*opposite, top*) Another undated view of Newbiggin station with G5 No.67341 at the head of a Manors service; the station appears uninspiring and the deserted platform with its archaic gas lights reflect something of a nation exhausted by six years of relentless war and even more years of austerity. Tickets issued here in 1951 amounted to 23,514, a far cry from the 165,927 issued forty years previously in 1911. Yes motor buses had wreaked havoc with the passenger numbers from the 1920s but Newbiggin was part of the Ashington group of coal mines which during the post-war years became some of the most productive in the land employing many thousands of men. BR's answer to the decline was to employ the diesel multiple units but although they started work here in 1958, the new units didn't make much difference to passenger numbers so the decline was halted by closing the passenger stations and withdrawing all services from 2nd November 1964. (*opposite*) No.67341 runs round its train; the G5 was allocated to South Blyth 16/10/55–7/7/57 when it transferred to Botanic Gardens and never returned to the north-east. That therefore puts these images inside the dates presented. Note the porter dropping the parcels and the guard taking no notice of his dilemma – team work eh! *Both J.W.Armstrong (ARPT).*

(*above*) A Metro-Camm two-car d.m.u. at Newbiggin during that final year of rail operations in 1964; the station had opened on 1st March 1872 but the place was now run-down; weeds have taken over the sidings and run-round track on the left, the fencing looks ready for burning! Note the slight inward curve built into the platform. Roy Stevens. (*below*) From about 1958 Newbiggin station had a Camping Coach located in the yard where coal wagons were once unloaded. This view of the 'holiday amenity' is taken from across the allotments on the south side of the station on 20th June 1959. This writer has little idea of the weekly 'going-rate' for the accommodation but although the vehicles were self-contained in most respects, the boarders had to use the station toilets for ablutions. Now just glance over that allotment at a piece of real estate with all its bits and bats cobbled together to illustrate perhaps in a nutshell the Britain of the immediate post-war years. Sentimental, me?! *Stoker Redfern LGC collection.*

(*above*) J27 No.65794 prepares to run back onto BR property from Woodhorn Colliery with a loaded coal train on 2nd June 1961. This train is headed for the staiths at North Blyth, virtually next door to where this 0-6-0 was allocated at North Blyth engine shed. Already 55-years old, the J27 would receive a General overhaul some seven months after this scene was captured. This mine remained productive until February 1981 and was the reason for keeping this section of the Newbiggin branch open. The branch was already working when Woodhorn pit started production in 1894. Now imagine how many tons of coal has passed over this stretch of the branch. (*below*) Ashington station with wall-to-wall diesel units circa 1960; the furthest unit is 'pegged' for Newbiggin. *Both Stoker Redfern LGC collection.*

An undated illustration of North Seaton station from the 'six-foot' in BR days looking north with the main buildings on the right and a simple wooden shed providing shelter for intending passengers on the other platform side. Access to North Seaton Colliery was behind the photographer and the viaduct shown opposite, top, was a little further on. Opened November 1859, this was a terminal until the line to Newbiggin was completed in March 1872. Closed 2nd November 1964, the goods facility closed in December 1963. Note that a train is due and the gates blocking the A196 are closed but note how they overlap. (*A tale of a North Seaton signalman on permanent nightshift was placed on double dayshift much to his disapproval. Unbeknown to the authorities he was partially sighted so on nights he could see the vehicles lights, when on days he locked a woman and pram inside the gates, Needless to say he was dismissed!*) *J.W.Armstrong Misc (E.Brack)*.

(*opposite, top*) Shades of summers past and present litter the shore of the River Wansbeck; an unidentified Q6 crosses North Seaton viaduct with empty coal hoppers from North Blyth power station to Ashington Colliery in 1965. This bridge replaced a timber viaduct – reputed to be the largest wooden structure in Britain at 400 yards long and 85ft high – in 1929. *Unknown photographer.* (*opposite*) Of similar lightweight design, Sleekburn viaduct spans the River Blyth near Bedlington. Also built in 1929, this structure too replaced another wooden viaduct dating from the 1850s. *J.W.Armstrong (ARPT)*.

With the locomotive crew looking on, G5 No.67326 takes water at Bedlington circa 1955, whilst working a Manors-Newbiggin service.
68 *J.W.Armstrong (ARPT)*.

Another G5, South Blyth's No.67341, takes water at Bedlington circa 1956 whilst working a service to Newbiggin. This was the junction of the lines to Morpeth – off to the left – and Ashington – to the right. The station here consisted just an island platform whereby bi-directional running took place on the Up side; the Down side platform face was a bay for trains from Newbiggin in the early days. *J.W.Armstrong* (*ARPT*). 69

En route to Ashington Colliery for another load of 'fulls', South Blyth based J27 No.65876 runs through Bedlington with the compulsory brake van on 22nd March 1963. The compact station building can be seen at the other end of the platform with quite a turn-out of intending passengers awaiting the next train. Just one year from the date of this photograph this locomotive was condemned and sent to Darlington for cutting-up! *Christopher Campbell.*

An ailing J27 No.65822, from South Blyth, runs (wheezes more like!) through Bedlington with mineral empties circa 1964. The station was serving 27,000 occupants of the town during LNER days, all down to one platform! The footbridge served the community until 1973 when it was demolished. *Malcolm Dunnett (ARPT)*.

Bedside (renamed April 1860) originally Cowpen Lane, opened June 1850 by the B&T. Closed 2nd November 1964 by BR. An undate
72 **view of the station with a southbound coal train being eased across the level crossing of the A193 Blyth road by a J27.** *J.W.Armstrong (ARPT)*